# A Fairy Tale of Love:
# The Jimmy & Georgie Story

JAMES MITCHELL SR.

Paul,
Thank you for
your support.
Jim Mitchell



PRINTED IN THE UNITED STATES OF AMERICA.



ISBN 979-8-9915948-1-3

PUBLISHED BY SMALL HOUSE PUBLISHING

# Contents

Chapter One

# How It All Began

I am writing at this time because I cannot sleep. I am so anxious to write this story, our story. A story that I love to tell. I call it a "Fairy Tale of Love." It all began during the winter of 1971 when my family moved from Hudson Street in New Haven to the Quinnipiac Terrance Housing Complex (the projects). We didn't know anyone living there but soon discovered everyone knew each other.

We were the new family, and we stood out. My brother Frank and I wore full-length leather coats. People were curious about the new kids on the block. They would see us walking up "The Hill" from our apartment on English Street to Downing Street as we made our way to the Cumberland Farms store on Ferry Street. This walk, which we did regularly, became known as the Cumberland Farms Walk because it was our way of exploring the neighborhood and getting to know the people and places around us.

Doreen Gore (Georgie) and her family lived on Downing Street. I often saw her outside in front of their apartment. It didn't take long for me to notice her. I would see her around, hanging with her posse, Bebe (Valerie Barber), Diane Johnson, and Lynn Mallory. She was the prettiest girl I had ever seen, and I wanted to meet her. It was tough to talk to her because her posse protected her like they were her secret service agents.

January 1972 was finally my chance. She was standing on her porch in front of their apartment alone. Georgie didn't look happy. I approached her, introduced myself, and asked her why she looked so sad. She replied, "It's my birthday, and I'm having a birthday party, but it isn't going well." It was a moment that tested my determination to win her heart.

"Don't worry. There will be many more birthdays, more birthday parties, and they will only get better," I told Georgie. She had just turned 13 years old. Shortly after, her mother pulled up in her car. "What are you doing?" she asked. I told her that I was trying to get to know her daughter. She sternly told me her daughter was too young to have a boyfriend, to which I replied, "I am not trying to be a boyfriend, just a friend." Her tone and disposition conveyed her desire for me to leave, which I did.

I remember walking away on a cloud. Georgie knew my name, and I knew hers. I got her attention, and she started pursuing me. However, because her mother disapproved of me, we could not be seen together near her home. We would sneak around and meet at the homes of friends.

Georgie was mature for her age and yet very innocent. She was feisty and beautiful, with the smoothest brown silk skin. She had a curvy figure for a girl her age. I understand why her mother wanted me to stay away from her. But these qualities attracted me to her, especially her feistiness. Whenever we were together, she would kick me with her hard platform shoes, scratch me all over my arms, or throw rocks at me. It was her way of being affectionate, and I loved it because I knew it meant she liked me. Once, my father saw the scratches and asked me what happened to my arms. I told him that I met a girl and that she had a cat. Georgie didn't have a cat; she was the cat!

We eventually solidified our relationship. It was the kind of innocent love that only young hearts can experience. She was my princess, and I was her knight in shining armor. We were young; she was 14 years old, and I was 17 years old, yet we knew we were made for each other. We were total opposites in our personalities, but we shared a lot in common. We were both the middle child in our families, liked music and liked to drive. I'm reminded of a party that we both attended. She brought some of her records to the party, and there was one song that I liked. The song was "I Miss You" by Harold Melvin & the Blue Notes. I liked the song because I missed her when we were apart, so I took the record.

Later, I discovered it belonged to her, so I returned it and told her I had borrowed it. She forgave me because I explained that this was our song. Then, there was the driving incident. Georgie had turned 15 years old, and I had just bought my first car. A 1964 Chevy Impala SS (Supersport, a classic) with a pull-out 8-track tape deck. During this time, I was accepted by her mother. She knew that we were "going together" and allowed it. I would park my car on The Hill across from where she lived. I would leave the keys with her so she could listen to the music on the 8-track while I played basketball in the park. Before I knew it, she was driving my car. She would circle the park (even though she didn't have a license). I don't know how she learned to drive.

One day, returning from her trip around the park and parking the car, she hit the curb and busted the front driver's side tire. She came to the park where I played basketball, threw the keys at me, and said, "Take these keys." It was a moment of frustration and misunderstanding. I didn't know what happened until I finished playing ball and went to get the car. There it sat with a flat tire, and it was my fault. It was a minor incident, but it reminded us of the challenges we faced in our relationship.

I was now a senior in high school and decided not to go to college. I enlisted in the Army. There was a program where you could sign up six months before graduation, and upon graduating you would leave for basic training. I wanted to leave as soon as I graduated before I started enjoying being out of school. I was afraid that If I didn't leave immediately, I would change my mind and not go. I decided to tell Georgie my plans. When I told her that I had joined the

Army, she replied, "You're going to leave me?" and started to cry. I explained to her that I wasn't going to college, the economy needed to be improved, and few jobs were available. I said that I had to do something with my life. She told me that she wanted to go with me. You see, she was not happy with her home life. She had five sisters living at home; for the longest, it was a house of all girls: her, the five sisters, and her mother, Ms Nancy.

Her mother had taken in a boyfriend (Mr. Louie), which disrupted the household dynamics. She resented having a stepfather. I told her to go with me, we would have to get married. She cried even more (after all, her astrological sign was Aquarius, the water bearer). But that was not why she cried. Georgie thought that I was messing with her. I told her I was serious and asked her if she wanted to get married. I never expected her to say yes, but she did. As I stated earlier, her maturity, not to mention her bravery, was incredible to agree to get married at 15 years ol.

Chapter Two

# The Two Become One + One

We were ready. All we had to do was get the marriage license and find a place for the wedding and the reception. However, planning a wedding was a problem because we needed more money. I had a part-time job after school, and Georgie sometimes worked with her stepfather doing office cleaning in the evening, but that wouldn't be enough to pay for a wedding. Yet, we knew we wanted to get married. Her mother said we could get married at her house, and my oldest sister, Big Lou, said we could hold the reception at her home on Orchard Street.

We had a venue for the wedding and the reception; we just had to work out the details. We got our marriage license from City Hall. We contacted Reverend Curtis Cofield, the Pastor of Immanuel Baptist Church, and asked him to officiate the ceremony. After counseling Georgie and I, he agreed to marry us. He understood our situation and genuine love for each other. I attended the church as a young man. My sister Big Lou offered to pay for the reception expenses as a wedding gift. We had Georgie's wedding dress made in New Haven. Georgie chose a yellow dress that accommodated her baby bump as she started to "grow and show." Georgie felt that she shouldn't get married in a white dress because a white dress symbolized innocence and virginal purity, and we had already been intimate. I asked my best friend Faustino (Faust) Lopez (my now brother-in-law) to be my best man, and Georgie's sister Mary "Rollie" Gore was her maid of honor. We chose June 15th as the date for the wedding. We were all set to tie the knot.

On June 15, 1974, Georgie, the best man, maid of honor, our parents, siblings, and I gathered at her mother's house for the ceremony. The ceremony took place in the living room. I remember it being a beautiful, sunny day. Georgie came out dressed in her lovely, specially made yellow dress. I thought, "What a beautiful bride." She was glowing with her smooth, silky, chocolate skin. I was wearing a powder blue suit I bought for my high school graduation, six days away. We weren't color-coordinated with the powder blue and yellow, but we didn't care. We were getting married!

The Reverend Curtis Cofield performed the beautiful ceremony, and now we were two hearts beating. I think I was glowing or at least joyful and delighted. We were now husband and wife.

## Chapter Three

# The Honeymoon

Now that we were married, Georgie was no longer my princess; she was now my queen, and I was her king. Usually, after the wedding, there is the honeymoon. However, there was nothing ordinary about our marriage because 15 & 18 year old teenagers don't typically get married right after high school.

That did not matter to us. We were married, and we were in love. Getting married was our honeymoon. The fact that we could pull off getting married was good enough for us. We walked away from our wedding with approximately $36.00 in our pockets—barely sufficient to buy a meal for two at McDonald's, but we didn't care.

After the wedding reception, I stayed with Georgie and her family at her mother's house. We knew it would be a short stay as I would graduate from Wilbur Cross High School soon and then report to basic training for the Army in thirteen days. We knew what we were in for and just wanted to be together as long as possible before my departure. The time went by quickly, too quickly. It was tough leaving, but we understood that we had to do it to be together from now, "until death do we part," as stated in our wedding vows. Did I tell you how strong and brave Georgie was?

I reported to basic training on June 28, 1974, at the Army training center at Fort Dix, New Jersey. The training was very intense, but I was in good physical shape. Being mentally tough helped me get through the training. I thought about my bride and the baby she was carrying every free mental break I got. The training kept me mentally occupied. However, I would call her whenever I got a chance.

I remember listening to Elton John's "Benny and the Jets" and the Ohio Players's "Skin Tight" album at night after the training day. Music has always been in my blood and helped me through tough times. I completed basic training in mid-September and came home for about a week before reporting to the second phase of my AIT (Advanced Individual Training) training in Aberdeen, Maryland. By this time, Georgie was much farther along in her pregnancy. Georgie loved that the baby was also kicking regularly. She would place my hand on her stomach and say, "Feel here. Did you feel him kick?" She knew that it was a boy. I told her that I felt him kick and that I believed that the baby was trying to kick his way out of her stomach because he knew I was home. The time for her to deliver the baby was fast approaching, and I knew she couldn't wait for it to happen. It had been a hot summer, and carrying a baby during those hot months (July and August) was no picnic; at least, that is what she told me. While doing my AIT training, I could come home on the weekends. I had an instructor at AIT who lived in Massachusetts and went home every weekend. He would let me catch a ride and drop me off on his way. He would pick me up on his way back to Aberdeen, MD, and all I had to do was split the cost of gas. Well, the day came for the baby to be delivered. It was Sunday, October 27, 1974.

Luckily, I was home that weekend, and our first son, James Jr., was born. I had to leave that night to return to my duty station. I remember being filled with so much joy. My firstborn child, Georgie, was his mother. I knew that she would make a great mom, and she did. We all had nicknames in my family.

So, I gave James Jr. the nickname "Snoog." One of my training instructors used a word to describe things. He would say, "You take this snooga booga and attach it to that snooga booga." It was catchy. That nickname still sticks after all these years.

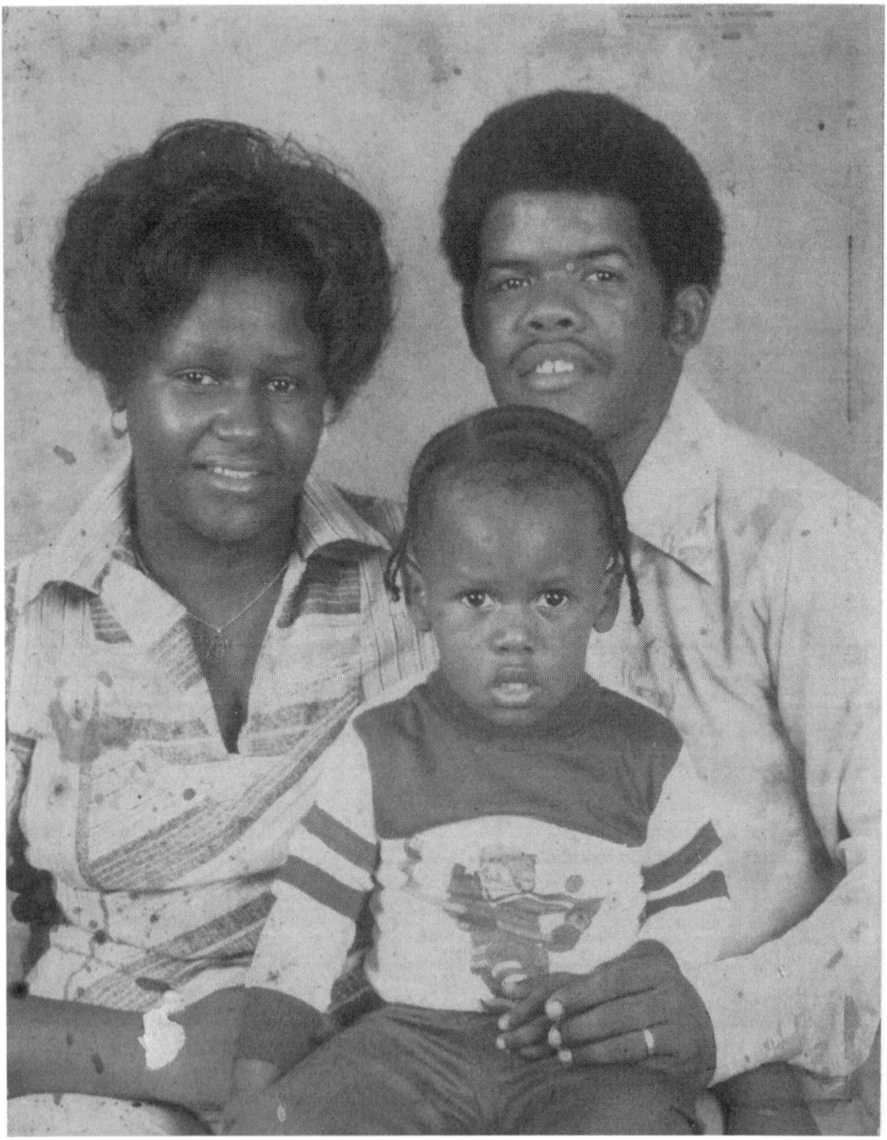

Chapter Four

# The Reunion

I completed the second training phase in December 1974 and was given two weeks of leave before reporting to my final duty station at Fort Hood, TX. I enjoyed spending time with my wife and my newborn son, Snoog. The time went by quickly, and in early January 1975, I boarded a plane en route to Fort Hood. Once I arrived and got settled in, I found us a furnished apartment in Killeen, TX., at 808 Sissom. Rd. I then purchased a plane ticket for Georgie and Snoog to come down to Texas and join me. She had never flown before and was taking her first plane ride alone with a newborn baby. But she did not hesitate. Georgie and Snoog arrived in Texas at Dallas-Fort Worth Airport, where I met them and took them to our new apartment. Did I mention how brave and strong Georgie was? She had just turned 16 years old. Now, we were indeed a family. Two hearts beating as one (plus one, Snoog).

Starting was challenging as we had no family to turn to for help. Often, I would be taken away from home to go to the field for Army training, anywhere from three to seven days at a time, leaving Georgie and Snoog all alone. I remember one time that I was going to the field, and a terrible rainstorm hit. Georgie was alone and afraid, so she called her mother. Her mother contacted the Red Cross. The next thing I knew, I was pulled off the truck I was driving, heading out to the field, and sent home. I was glad. After my unit returned home from the field, three days later, I was told that the storm was so bad that it knocked down the tents. I was lucky that I wasn't in the field. I was home in the comfort of our house with my family, and all was well, or so I thought.

Georgie and I were learning what it meant to be a married couple with adult responsibilities. One night, Georgie attempted to make instant mashed potatoes, but they came out watery, not mashed. She started crying. "I don't know how to cook," Georgie sobbed. She was an Aquarius astrological sign, the water bearer. They cry often. I knew she could cook as she spent much time in the kitchen watching her mother. "Why are you making instant mashed potatoes? I know you can cook." I encouraged her to cook like she did when she lived with her mother. Georgie turned out to be a great cook, and we had the weight gain to prove it! Georgie also turned out to be a great mother and wife. Our love just continued to flourish.

Though we were content with our new life as a married couple and young family, Georgie started feeling homesick. She wanted to return to New Haven, CT, to visit her mother and siblings. I agreed and bought her a plane ticket so she and Snoog could go home for two weeks. She went home but only stayed for one week, as she quickly realized that her "home" was with me and our small family in Texas. I purchased her a return ticket so they could return home to Killeen, and she never left me again. Did I tell you how loyal Georgie was?

Chapter Five

# End of Time in Service

The following two and a half years were spent in Killeen, Texas, while I completed my military service. It was a fun time. We met many people who, like us, were there because of the military. We made friends from all over the country with different cultural backgrounds. Most of us were from the same Army unit, the 124th Maintenance Battalion, 2nd Armor Division. We were all family.

The time went by quickly. My ETS (end of time in service) date was approaching, and I contemplated re-enlisting but decided against it. Instead, I decided to change careers from maintenance mechanic/clerk to pursue a new career in the medical field. I chose not to re-enlist in the military because the military tends to separate families if a soldier is assigned to a different duty station.

On June 27, 1977, I was given my discharge papers. Before I was discharged, however, I joined the CT Army National Guard. When I returned home, I was to report as a part-time soldier to the 142nd Medical Battalion in New Haven, Connecticut. I saved some unused leave time to cash in for pay. With my final month's salary and the money from the leave I cashed in, we left Fort Hood with about $4000.00, which would be our seed money for starting our new life when we returned to New Haven.

I had a 1968 Buick GS400, which was not in the best mechanical condition. I had it checked by a mechanic who assured me it was in good enough condition to make the 1,800-mile trip home. We took our time driving, stopping along the way. We drove 575 miles before the car started giving us trouble. A line to the transmission broke, and we stopped in Sulfur Springs, Arkansas, to see if we could get the car fixed.

Sulfur Springs did not appear to be a town that welcomed African Americans. Georgie felt very uncomfortable and wanted to leave as soon as possible. I found an automotive shop and asked them if they could repair the car. They said they could, but it would take three days. We were not going to stay in that hick town for three days. We felt we would never be heard from again if we did. I asked the mechanic if he would buy the car for the bus ticket cost so we could be on our way. He agreed and gave us $300.00 for the car. The three of us got the hell out of Sulfur Springs. The trip home by bus took three days, but we didn't care as long as we didn't have to spend one night in Sulfur Springs, Arkansas. After such a long trip, we needed a shower when we arrived in New Haven, but we were home and together, which is what mattered to us most.

Chapter Six

# The Transition

It is April 4, 2024, at 3:30 AM. Once again, I am unable to sleep. I need to continue writing and telling Georgie's story, our story. I want to finish writing this book by the first anniversary of Georgie's death, May 30th. I will continue.

We arrived in New Haven in early July 1977. It had been a long, grueling three-day bus ride, and we couldn't wait to get to Georgie's mother's house to shower and sleep. Well, at least shower because we knew everyone would be happy to see us and have lots to discuss.

We took it easy for the first few days as we made plans to find a job and an apartment and check in with my National Guard unit. Things went smoothly. My brother-in-law, Faustino Lopez, was a maintenance mechanic at a nearby factory. He was able to get me a job there at Interstate Container Corp. I started immediately. The job was convenient because it was within walking distance and I didn't have a car. It turned out to be a sweatshop where the temperature was well over 100 degrees daily. The factory needed high temperatures and heat to produce the corrugated boxes. Huge boilers provided the heat. We had big fans at our workstations to offer some relief from the heat, which didn't provide much relief, especially during the summer months. I didn't mind because it was a job, a starting point. It turned out to be a fun place to work. There were "old heads" who worked there and they were quite the characters. Preston Little, Foster "Hot Papa" Robinson, Jimmy Mack, Curtis Stewart, and Ike "Nub" Benton (named "Nub" because part of his right arm was amputated), to name a few. They've all passed on, but they were a fun bunch to work with. The job allowed Georgie and I to get on our feet.

We got an apartment in the Quinnipiac Housing Complex (the projects) at 119 Downing Street, behind Georgie's mother's house. Being a military veteran helped us get the apartment within a month of returning home due to military preference. I used the money from my final paycheck from my discharge from the Army, which allowed us to buy furniture from a local furniture store. We furnished the apartment on credit. Georgie and I also purchased our first car, a 1972 Buick 225. It was a great car! It was big like a caddy, rode like a caddy, and guzzled gas like a caddy. But that didn't matter because, during this time, gas was pretty cheap. Gas was about .62 per gallon then.

We were on our way, transitioning to the next chapter. Initially, Georgie was a stay-at-home mom, caring for our only son, James Jr. We were adjusting to our new civilian life. I was working at Interstate Container and reporting to the National Guard one weekend a month. Georgie went back to school to get her High School diploma. She dropped out of school after completing the tenth grade to come and live with me in Texas. Georgie attended classes at the Q House on Dixwell Avenue, took the GED test, and passed. She was very proud of the accomplishment, and I was very proud and happy for her. Georgie was very determined!

After getting her GED, Georgie went to work at the local McDonalds. She would work there for about a year until she got pregnant with our second son, Jermell Allen (Bucks). Bucks was born on January 30, 1979, and Georgie, once again, was a stay-at-home mom. I completed my two-year obligation in the CT Army National Guard and decided to get out to spend more time with the family. However, I had to take on a second part-time job to compensate for the lost wages. I enrolled in a trade school, Technical Careers Institute, attending classes in the evening in their Automotive Mechanic program. Upon completing the course, I started looking for an automotive mechanic job. To get an entry level mechanics position, I would have to take a pay cut, so I stayed at Interstate Container to get an entry-level mechanics job. Soon after, they announced the plant was closing. That was music to my ears as it forced me now to find a job as a mechanic. I eventually found a job as a contractor for the Grumman Company bus division. The Grumman Company built new buses to replace the aging fleet of buses in New York, Connecticut, and several other states. However, before the buses were road tested to see if they would hold up on the New York streets, the city of New York convinced the Gruman Company to sell them the buses. New York agreed to pay half the cost for any problems that arose. Well, there were many problems!

The bus frames were built out of aluminum and did not hold up on the roads of New York. The engines started falling out, the frames cracked, and the buses had to be retrofitted with steel plates and metal frames. It was a big undertaking and an excellent opportunity for employment as the work was being done in Hamden on Welton Street, just down the street from the Hamden Motor Vehicle Department. I was hired as a mechanic and worked there for about 3-4 years with unlimited overtime. It was an opportunity to make some good money as the pay was pretty good. While working there, I met a gentleman in the Army Reserve. We talked about my time in the military and what I had going for retirement. I had nothing planned for retirement. He got my attention, and it got me thinking about my future. So, in May of 1983, I joined the CT Army National Guard again. I would do 34 years in the National Guard and retire with a pension and free medical benefits. The job with Grumman Company was winding down, and I got a mechanics job with Tri-Lift Inc., a forklift rental, sales, and service company in East Haven. I grew to hate the job as I was the only minority in the company and became the dumping ground for all their dirty work and the scapegoat for everything that went wrong. After working there for a few years, I was given my walking papers and laid off for lack of work.

Again, I was the scapegoat for problems with the maintenance of the forklifts. I didn't care because I was glad to be out of there. However, Georgie was now pregnant with our third son. I negotiated a deal for medical coverage with Tri-Lift to cover the birth of Jamar Andre (Scooch), born on March 20, 1983. Tri-Lift agreed because they knew my termination was invalid as there was plenty of work. I was not laid off for any performance issues, and when I went to pick up my toolbox, a new hire was bringing his toolbox in. I didn't care. I was just glad to be out of that toxic environment. I decided to return to school for the Electronic Technician course at the Connecticut School of Electronics in New Haven. I also worked the third shift at Spectra-Strip Cable Company in Hamden so I could attend school during the day.

The federal government paid for all my schooling as a benefit, for the time that I served in the U.S. Army. I completed my two-year certificate course, and upon graduation, I landed my first corporate job at Digital Equipment Corporation, a computer company based in Hudson, Massachusetts. It was the best job that I ever had. I was a field service technician, going from business to business and repairing computers. The job paid well, had great benefits, and a company car. This job provided us with the means to move out of the projects.

Meanwhile, Georgie went back to work. One day, she told me that she wanted to quit her job. I asked her why, and she said so she could stay home and raise our kids. I told her we needed a second income, to which she replied, "Well then, you better get a second job."

I did get another job in addition to my job at Digital Equipment Corp (DEC) and the National Guard. It was her best move as she ensured our sons were correctly raised. Georgie eventually returned to the workforce once Snoog and Bucks could fend for themselves. She took a job as the Head Cook for the YWCA daycare. It was beneficial because Georgie could take Scooch with her and enroll him in the daycare. They were lucky to have her; she was an excellent cook, and they could not get enough of her cooking.

Eventually, we could buy our first house on Ferry Street in New Haven. It was a two-family house with an unfinished attic. We remodeled the house and finished the attic. It was its own apartment, without a kitchen and bathroom, but it was Snoog and Buck's apartment. Eventually, two of Georgie's nieces, Charlene (Mini) and Chanine (Sophia), would come and live with us for a while, as would Georgie's nephew Corey. We were one big happy family.

Chapter Seven

# Our Family

Our family was now complete. When we married and talked about how many kids we wanted, Georgie said she wanted three boys. She said that girls were too much trouble to raise. I figured Georgie, from a family of eight girls, knew what she was talking about. So, her wish was granted. We had our three sons (plus nephew Corey). And besides, her two nieces, Charlene and Chanine, who stayed with us for some time, were like our daughters.

I felt incredibly proud of our family unit and how we raised our kids. They all turned out well and became very successful. They all, including our nieces and nephews, did exceptionally well in school before college, for which I credit Georgie. I played a big part in their success, but Georgie was no-nonsense, especially regarding the kid's education. We were a great team. She is the disciplinary one, and I am the male role model and mentor. She always had the kids with her, no matter where she went. I spent much time on the road either working, traveling for job training, or away in the National Guard. When I was away, she filled in my role. She taught the boys how to play baseball, drove them to baseball practice, and got them to all their games. When Scooch decided to play football, she again filled in by playing catch with him and getting him to practice. Nothing came between her and the kids.

As with any marriage, ours was not perfect. There were some hurtful times, and some pain was shared. Some were self-inflicted, and some were pains that we inflicted on each other. But it only served to make us stronger, and it brought us closer together. Our home was filled with love and happiness. We always had a house full of kids, our immediate and extended family. The friends and classmates of our kids were always welcome to come over after school and hang out. You didn't just hang out and do whatever you wanted. There was structure and discipline, and many kids welcomed it. They needed discipline. And if you came over and spent time there, you were fed a good meal. When our kids, including their friends, sometimes got out of line, Georgie would "go off." Everybody would scatter, but before you knew it, they all returned like nothing happened.

The fact that we provided such a caring, loving, and nurturing environment for so many made us happy. It brought us great joy to provide a safe environment for the kids to come to and not have to hang out in the streets. Everyone called Georgie "Mom" or "Weezey," and I was and still am "Pops." So many kids would come over and hang out that I couldn't keep up with them. Today, I run into some of them when I'm out and about, and I have no idea who they are, but they all know me. They would say, "You're Snoog, Bucks, or Scooch's father." And Georgie, she knew every last one of them. They still come by the house during cookouts, special occasions or to stop by and say hello. And they show nothing but respect and love. Did I mention how much Georgie was loved?

Chapter Eight

# Music Lovers

It's hard to pick just one song that Georgie and I liked. We both loved music, and we had so many favorites. But Brian McKnight was one of Georgie's favorite artists. His song, "The Love of My Life," Was a constant in our lives. I remember the first time I heard it with Georgie; we were driving to the beach, the wind in our hair and the music filling the car. It was a perfect moment. I took Georgie to Brian McKnight's concert, and she was so thrilled when he sang this song. What a fantastic night seeing her so happy.

There are so many other moments. Georgie would drive around with our three sons in her Brown Honda Accord with the music blasting, listening to the sounds of late 80's and early 90's Hip Hop and R&B. Amongst some of the favorite songs to listen to with the windows down were "Overweight Lover" by Heavy D, "New Jack Swing" by Wreckx-n-Effect, and "I'm Dreamin" by Christopher Williams. Regardless of our destination, if any of those songs or others that were popular during that era came on, two things would be guaranteed: we'd continue driving around until the song came to a completion, and we'd all be singing the music at the top of our lungs as we enjoyed our travels. The icing on the cake during our mobile karaoke parties came about as we approached our home neighborhood. A particular intersection allowed us a little hang time as we approached it, going above the speed limit. For that split second, it seemed we were floating above the street as our favorite songs played. This maneuver, which we called the "doonk," was named by our youngest son, Scooch. He said that was the car's sound when we completed our jump. This memory will forever be etched in our childhood summer activities.

We have been into music ever since our days in the Army. We brought albums every time we got paid. Georgie and I developed quite a collection of albums and LP singles. We loved music; today, we still have about twelve crates of albums from back in the day. We had a setup in our house with two turn tables and a mixer. We were want-to-be DJs. I was "DJ Brown Sugar," and Georgie was "DJ Weezy." We had a lot of fun with our music and always threw house parties. We dreamed of playing at significant events and making people dance to our music. Music was a big part of our lives and is still so today. Music is very relaxing. It soothes your body and soul and escapes your daily challenges. Music is therapeutic and we were true music lovers.

Chapter Nine

# Preparing the Kids for Life

It's the late 1980s. The foundation of our family was all set, and we were cruising along life on auto-pilot. We focused on ensuring our kids got the most out of school. Our sons were four years apart, so they covered the three levels of education in public school. Snoog was in high school, and we were focused on ensuring he had the best opportunity to attend college, as Georgie and I did not.

Snoog would be the first in our family to go to college and pave the way for his brothers to follow. Snoog attended Career High (formerly known as Richard C. Lee High). Career High prepares students for a career in the workforce, focusing on a business major, or the opportunity to attend any college in the country, of their choosing. Career High had an outstanding faculty and staff led by Principal Williams. Snoog was enrolled in all advanced AP college preparatory classes, and the teachers at Career High pushed the students to maximize their full potential. Snoog was exceptional. Upon graduation, he attended The University of Connecticut (UConn). He had a very successful, enjoyable, and memorable college career. In college, he met many friends and family who became part of our extended family. They still stay in touch today and get together regularly. Friends like Natalie, Thais,

Amarilis, Shank, Ralph, and Al, to name a few. After graduating, Snoog held many jobs, eventually settling in at Comcast/Xfinity. He would marry Tina Couvertier, and they have two children (Zamara and Xavier). They currently reside in Wallingford, CT.

Next up was Jermell (Bucks), who also attended Career High and would follow in Snoog's footsteps and attend UConn. Bucks attended UConn for two years before a medical issue caused him to take a break and attend to his health. He would return to college and attend Louisiana State University in Baton Rouge, Louisiana. He eventually moved to San Diego, CA where he resides today.

Bucks has held various sales positions in the Financial Tech (FinTech) sector. Bucks also met his wife, Mallory Serbin, in San Diego, and they have a son (Asher). Last up is Jamar (Scooch), the baby of the bunch. Scooch followed his two brothers and attended Career High but took a different path to college. Jamar attended Moorehouse College, an HBCU (Historically Black College and University) in Atlanta. After graduating, he met and married Monique Garrett, and they have two children (Savannah and Spencer). After living in Marlboro, Massachusetts, for a few years, they moved to Fort Worth, Texas, where they lived for several years before eventually returning to Connecticut and settling in Hamden.

Now that our family was established and our sons were grown, married, and off and running in their prospective careers, it was time for Georgie and I to focus on us. What were our dreams and hopes, and how would we achieve them? I still served in the CT Army National Guard and worked for Digital Equipment Corp\Compaq\Hewlett Packard. The three computer companies had undergone mergers and were now known as Hewlett Packard Corp. I worked there for twenty years until December 2005. The computer industry was transforming, and companies started to downsize. I was allowed to take a buyout with a good severance package. I took the package, left, and worked for the NCR Corporation, a significant computer service organization focusing on retail and financial services. I worked there for fourteen years before retiring in November 2019. I retired from the National Guard in September 2015 after serving thirty-seven years (three years of Active Duty and thirty-four years in the National Guard).

Georgie had now gone to work for Yale-New Haven Hospital in the food service sector. She worked there for about twenty years before retiring in 2016 due to medical issues. Her medical condition now highlighted our need to move from Ferry Street and pursue our dream of owning a one-family house. Georgie was starting to have problems with her knees, and living on the second floor presented a challenge. We started looking for a ranch-style house with all the rooms on a single level. We came across a lovely two-bedroom ranch home on Federal Street during our search. It had been well-maintained and updated with a fully finished basement. It wasn't a large house, but it was just the right size for us. It had excellent curb appeal, and we immediately knew it suited us. Federal Street is a tranquil street in the Benham St. and Circular Ave area, a far cry from the noisy, busy life of Ferry Street. We bid for the Federal Street home, which was accepted and moved in September 2015.

Federal Street was now our retirement home, though I didn't fully retire. I went to work part-time for a non-profit organization. I started working for Concepts for Adaptive Learning in November 2019 after retiring from NCR Corp. Concept for Adaptive Learning (CfAL), a non-profit computer company that provides basic computer training for marginalized families. After completing the training, the family receives a refurbished donated computer for their household.

SWING
FENCES

Chapter Ten

# It's All About Grandma

As we entered the next phase of our lives, often called "the golden years," we focused on the grandkids. Georgie loved kids, and now that our kids were grown, married, and establishing their own families, Georgie was looking forward to becoming a grandmother. She would get her wish very soon.

First came Zamara, born to our oldest son, James Jr., and his beautiful wife, Tina. Zamara was born on April 14, 2007. She was our first grandchild, and Georgie was ecstatic. The fact that our first grandchild was a girl, and we didn't have any daughters, just added to her happiness. Of course, being the first and only grandchild, we spoiled Zamara. We watched her grow from a little angel to Zamy, the tiny tot, into a precious little princess. Zamara loved spending time with her grandmother; they bonded as she grew.

Then came Xavier. Xavier was born two years later. We immediately knew he was special because of his independent, I-can-do-it-myself attitude. Xavier was our first grandson, and Georgie often referred to him as our oldest grandson once our other grandkids were born. This was to establish him as the male leader of the grandkids. Xavier exhibited my spirit. He was funny and loved dancing, as documented in his Friday video series, "Freaky Fridays." He also showed that he was quite an athlete at a very early age. From playing basketball to baseball to ice skating and becoming a hockey star in his own right, there was no sport that he could not master and excel in. Xavier also took up the sport of lacrosse, a non-traditional sport for people of color. Xavier was the only freshman to make the Varsity Lacrosse team. This is a further testament to his athleticism and hockey talents.

Zamara and Xavier loved coming to grandma's house for dinner, especially on Friday night when she would fix their favorite meal: Grandma's fried chicken with macaroni and cheese and broccoli. Xavier became the "taste-tester" and would let Grandma know when the broccoli had just the right amount of garlic powder sprinkled on it for just the right taste.

Also, one of their favorite pastime activities was singing along with Grandma as she sang their favorite songs. She would change the song's words to her version of the song. Boy, did they get a kick out of her version. It would just crack them up. Spending time with the grandkids was the highlight of our life. Georgie would light up whenever they came over, and I loved messing with Xavier. He would run to Grandma to complain and tell on me. They kept us going and young while we tried to keep up with them. Once they went home, Georgie and I would sit back and recap the events that took place during their visit or stay over, and we would laugh and laugh and laugh at all the funny things the two of them said and did. Ou grandkids brought much happiness to our lives. Georgie was glowing with joy. Georgie always had a glow, but with the grandkids as part of our family, her glow radiated even brighter than the sun's shining rays. Did I mention how beautiful Georgie was? She was gorgeous, and I just admired her beauty. I would often sit and stare at her. She would catch me staring and ask me why I was staring, to which I replied, "I am admiring your beauty and thinking about how much I loved you."

It wasn't long before our next two grandkids were born. Next came our second granddaughter, Savannah, born to our youngest son, Jamar, and his lovely wife, Monique. Jamar and his family were living in Fort Worth, Texas, at this time, and Georgie and I flew down to Texas to meet Savannah and help take care of her. Nothing could stand in the way of Georgie and our grandkids. Savannah's signature is her stare. Savannah will look at you if she doesn't want to be bothered and stare at you as if you aren't even there.

Spencer, our fourth grandchild, was born two years later. We took the trip to Fort Worth, Texas, to meet Spencer, the family's latest bundle of joy. Spencer, like Xavier, has that "I can do it by myself" attitude and is always in competition with his sister Savannah. As always with the little ones, I would mess with Spencer and get under his skin. Spencer would run and say, "Ganma," as he affectionately called her. He would tell "Ganma" that Pop-pop was being mean and urge her to "beat him up." We always got such a chuckle out of him.

Lastly, our fifth grandchild, Asher, was born. He was born to our middle son, Jermell, and his lovely wife, Mallory. Asher followed suit with the independent male trait exhibited by Xavier and Spencer. He is quite the charming little fellow and developed a love for exotic cars at the age of three. Asher and Spencer have an extensive vocabulary, and we are always amazed at the things they say.

We were blessed with five beautiful grandkids who always showed us how much they loved their grandparents. They always asked to come to grandma's house. It was always all about Grandma. The grandkids loved staying overnight. When Savannah and Spencer stayed overnight, they would insist on sleeping with "Ganma" in "Ganma's bed," and I had to sleep in the other bedroom. There was no negotiating; this is how it was. Our grandkids brought so much joy to our lives that they ruled us within reason. However, Georgie was big on discipline, and no one, not even me, challenged her on this principle.

Happy
Anniversary

Chapter Eleven

# The Final Chapter

Georgie and I were cruising in the middle lane down the highway of life. It was 2023, and we were living our best life. Georgie was content with her retirement, and I was semi-retired. I had retired from corporate America and now worked for a non-profit organization. Life was good. Our love for each other flourished as we spent more time together. We were approaching our forty-ninth wedding anniversary, and I was planning something special to celebrate. We also looked forward to traveling once Georgie had her knee replacement surgery. Her surgery was initially scheduled for early May but had to be rescheduled to July.

I looked forward to her knee replacement surgery. I was tired of seeing her in pain. I wanted to take care of her. "Why are you looking forward to taking care of me?" Georgie asked. I told her she had cared for me for forty-nine years, and now it was time for me to reciprocate. I also wanted her to resume an active life once she was healthy. I went with Georgie to her pre-opt physical, and all was well to move forward with the surgery.

We passed the time waiting for the surgery by spending as much quality time as we could with our grandkids. Zamara and Xavier's birthdays were in April, and Savannah and Spencer's were in May. Asher's birthday was in January, and because he lived in San Diego and Georgie could not travel, she at least got to Facetime with Asher. This made Georgie happy, as she wanted to be a part of all our grandkids' lives. Did I mention how much Georgie loved our grandkids?

While we prepared for Georgie's knee replacement surgery, we attended a pre-opt class to learn what to expect. The class taught us what would occur before, during, and after the surgery. We were told what to do physically and mentally to be in the best state in preparation for the operation. We were informed of the equipment needed during the recovery process. I purchased everything Georgie was told she would need before the procedure. I wanted to be prepared. Also, I wanted the recovery to be as short and painless as possible. Georgie was handling the time leading up to the surgery well. She had been through so many operations that this was routine for her.

All was going well until Thursday, May 25, 2023. Georgie nonchalantly said she felt like she might be coming down with something. She said that her throat felt a little "scratchy." Savannah and Spencer were coming over to spend the night as this was becoming our weekend routine, and nothing trumped that. "Are you feeling any better?" I asked. Georgie responded that she was ok, but something didn't feel right. As a precaution, I gave her a home COVID-19 test, which returned negative. The grandkids came over, and it was a typical evening. When it was time for bed, Savannah and Spencer climbed into Ganma's bed and chased me out of the room. They were hyped up and didn't want to sleep, so Georgie and I went back into the bedroom and tried to calm them down. We eventually got them to go to sleep. But, before I went to bed, I noticed Georgie was sluggish. I encouraged her to get in bed, thinking she was just tired. She did her usual routine of straightening up the house before bed.

I rose early, around 6:00 AM on Saturday morning, to make breakfast as always when the grandkids stayed over. Today was a special day. Savannah's birthday party was taking place later that afternoon. It wasn't long before the kids woke up excited. Georgie got up to help me feed the kids and get them dressed. Georgie said she wasn't feeling well enough to attend the birthday party. Georgie encouraged me to go and take Savannah's birthday present. She went back to bed and rested.

"Are you sure you're ok?" I asked. She insisted that she was alright and that I attend the birthday party. We thought she might be coming down with the flu, and rest would be best. I agreed to go.

I went to the party and stayed a little longer than I planned. I met and hung out with the fathers of the kids in attendance. We went for drinks at a local pub around the corner from the party venue and engaged in some fascinating conversation. I don't remember what time it was when I left. On the way home, I called to check on Georgie but didn't get an answer. I figured she was sleeping. When I arrived home, Georgie was asleep and had a slight fever. I took her temperature, gave her some Advil, put cold compresses on her to reduce the fever, and monitored her temperature. Her temperature returned to normal, and she went back to sleep. I joined her, and we both slept through the night.

I got up early the following day, hoping Georgie was feeling better. We planned to take Savannah and Spencer to the Hamden Memorial Day Parade. I was excited about taking them to the parade because they had never been. I bought them a fold-up lawn chair and an American flag to wave during the parade. But first, I had to make sure that Georgie was alright. She wasn't. She was unable to stay up and had to keep lying down. I brought Georgie a glass of ginger ale and tried to get her to eat some chicken noodle soup. I even tried feeding her. I sat on the bed beside her, and she laid her head on my shoulder. She looked at me and said, "Jimmy, I just don't feel good." It broke my heart. I looked into her eyes. Something just didn't feel right. I said, "Georgie, we must get you to the hospital immediately." Georgie was still in her pajamas, so I just put a coat on her. I backed the car around to the back door. We got her in the car and took off.

Georgie moaned the whole ride to the hospital. I pulled up to the emergency room entrance and had security bring a wheelchair. We got Georgie into the wheelchair, and they wheeled her into the emergency room while I parked the car. When I went inside, the nurse at the front desk took Georgie's temperature and remarked that her body temperature was low; it was only 84 degrees. She said to rush her into the Trauma Center. They made me wait in the emergency room to check her in. After about fifteen minutes, I could join her in the Trauma Center. When I walked into the Trauma Center, Georgie's backside was uncovered. It upset me to see this as I felt it was disrespectful to both of us.

A male nurse entered the room to take Georgie upstairs for more tests. I asked him what her temperature was. He said it was normal. I told him the nurse at the triage desk took Georgie's temperature when we came in, and it was 84 degrees. The nurse snapped back, "Well, I took it rectally, and it is normal." His attitude infuriated me. Now, I knew why her rear end was exposed. I wanted to go off on him, but I needed him to get her upstairs for the tests as quickly as possible. I waited in the Trauma Center until Georgie returned to the emergency room. A different nurse brought her back down. The good news was that Georgie wasn't having a stroke. She was dehydrated. The nurse was starting Georgie on some electrolytes, potassium, and antibiotics. She assured me the doctor would be in shortly. I waited about forty minutes, but the doctor never stopped in.

I asked the nurse how my wife was doing, and she said that Georgie was resting comfortably. I asked if she would be alright while I stepped into the waiting room to warm up. It was freezing. I stepped out and headed to check on a family that checked in at the same time we did. I was concerned about how their loved one was doing. When I tried to return to Georgie's room, I was detained. I was told that they were attending to my wife. I was unsure of what was happening. The hospital staff was vague with their communication. I later found out that Georgie went into cardiac arrest. After about thirty minutes, I was allowed back into the Emergency Room, but Georgie was no longer in her room. She was taken to the ICU.

I rushed upstairs to the ICU and was greeted by the attending physician. He told me what he thought had happened because he was not there. He said that Georgie went into cardiac arrest. He then said that it took the doctor twenty-five minutes to stabilize her. The nurse believed that Georgie vomited, swallowed it, and aspirated. I couldn't believe what I was hearing. I was stunned, in shock. I asked if she would be ok and was told the next twenty-four hours would be critical. Georgie was lying in the hospital bed unconscious, with all sorts of medical equipment hooked up to her. There were also many IV lines inserted into her. I was totally dumbfounded. I couldn't believe what I saw. I brought my wife into the hospital to be helped and treated for what I thought was the flu, and now she is lying on her deathbed.

How could this have happened? A doctor came and spoke with me. He said that they were going to give her an EEG (electroencephalogram) monitor to monitor her for seizures. He explained that this was routine for a patient who went through a very traumatic experience, as Georgie had, cardiac arrest. While this may be true, I felt that they were also monitoring her brain waves and brain activity to see if she was still alive. The other life support machines that were connected to Georgie were a ventilator to help her breathe, a device that kept her body temperature-controlled and stable, and an ECG to monitor her heart and vital signs. They led me to believe (or maybe that's what I wanted to believe) that she would be ok.

Three hours later, the attending doctor told me Georgie wasn't doing well. Her kidneys were not functioning correctly. The medical team requested to connect Georgie to a dialysis machine with my permission. I replied, "Do whatever you need to do. Just save my wife." When the dialysis machine was connected, it appeared to be working, but suddenly, her blood pressure started to drop. The doctors had to disconnect the dialysis machine. There wasn't anything else they could do. They couldn't just let her die. The doctor said he was sorry and left the room. I couldn't believe it, Georgie is dying.

I sat beside our niece, who was an on-duty nurse. She had been there watching everything closely from the time we arrived. I asked her if she heard what the doctor told me. She did. I was in disbelief. I was numb and in a state of shock. I felt helpless but hopeful as I watched the nurse working franticly, changing the IV bags. I went over to her and asked what she was doing and why. What was the outcome that she was hoping to achieve? Was there still hope? The doctor alluded to me that the end was near and that there was nothing more they could do. Another nurse responded to me, "I will do everything that I can to save your wife." I stood beside my wife, holding her hand and praying to God. I begged God not to let her die.

The doctor decided to try the dialysis machine once more. The nurse reconnected the machine, but Georgie's blood pressure dropped again. Her organs were failing. The medical team disconnected the dialysis machine as I stood holding Georgie's hand, praying. I looked at the ECG monitor and watched Georgie's blood pressure drop like a rock. She took her last breath, and she was gone. She never regained consciousness. I didn't get to say goodbye and tell her how much I loved her. Georgie was pronounced dead on March 30, 2023, at 5:50 AM. There were so many things that I needed to say to her. I kept repeating, "I love you. I love you. I will always love you." This was the end, or was it?

Chapter Twelve

# Georgie Lives On

As I wrote this book, the last chapter was the most difficult. Reliving the events and the memories of that dreadful Memorial Day weekend was very painful and emotional. It feels like it was yesterday, and the memories are very vivid. When I lost my beautiful wife, Georgie, I struggled with grief and the different stages. Denial, guilt, and acceptance were the most difficult ones. Denial: How could she be gone? How could this have happened? Guilt: I blamed myself. I was supposed to save Georgie, and I couldn't. Acceptance: I couldn't accept this. This was not supposed to happen.

I plunged into a deep state of depression. I was lost. When Georgie died, she took part of me with her. I lost my sense of purpose. I lost my identity. I didn't know what to do or where to turn. I had an incredible village of friends, family, and professional people who were there to support me and help me through this tough time. I was already seeing a therapist at the VA Hospital for some personal issues. We were about to end our treatment, and then suddenly, Georgie died. Now, I needed therapy in the worst way, so our sessions continued. My therapist helped me deal with this traumatic experience with much compassion and empathy. The therapy sessions really helped me to cope with my loss and my emotions and helped me talk about my feelings. I quickly realized how much I needed to tell Georgie's story, our story.

In addition to my village and my therapist, the church helped me tremendously. When Georgie died, and I was lost, I remembered something my father once told me. My father said," Son, if you ever get lost and don't know where to turn, you can always call on the Lord." I drew back on what my father said. These words were stuck in my head, waiting to be heard. I turned to Immanuel Missionary Baptist Church for guidance. The church welcomed me with open arms, and I immediately felt at home. The Pastor, Reverend Ross-Lee, is a great leader. His sermons helped me in a way that I am so grateful for. His messages resonated with me. I took the messages from Reverend Ross-Lee's sermons and executed them. He delivered one message: "When you're going through something, you must go through it. You can't go over it. You can't go under it or around it. You have to go through it." I heard that message and went through what I had to endure. I came out better, stronger, and with a different outlook. I now knew what I had to do.

I realized this was not the end but another chapter in our lives. I knew I had to keep Georgie's memories alive, tell her story, and allow her memory to live on by fulfilling her dream.

Georgie was very passionate about battered women and abused children. I knew I had to do something for that cause to honor her. I immediately went to a non-profit organization that ran a shelter for battered women and kids. I told them my story and asked what I could do to honor my lovely wife, Georgie. They asked me what I had in mind. I didn't know what I wanted to do, but I knew I needed to do something. I asked them what they needed? They suggested I help raise enough money to pay the security deposit and a month's rent to get a family out of the shelter and into a place they could call home, that it would be a great way to honor my wife and fulfill her dream. I loved the idea. I accepted the challenge.

I told my sons my wishes. I asked for their help, and they agreed and supported the idea. Things started slowly as my sons figured out how we could do this legitimately. We had to form a foundation and register it. I wondered if we could do it, as a lot of work and administrative requirements had to be done. I wanted to know if this would really come to fruition. Georgie's birthday, January 28th, was fast approaching, and I wanted to have something in place to announce a memorial fund in her honor. I didn't know what was going to happen. My sons, Snoog, Bucks, and Scooch, were working on this, even though I didn't realize it. I was planning a birthday party to honor and celebrate Georgie's birthday, to be held on January 27th, a day before her actual birthday. When Georgie was a little girl, her mother told her that her birthday was January 27th. So, for years, we celebrated Georgia's birthday on the 27th until she had to send for her birth certificate to get her passport. Well, what a surprise. Georgie's birth certificate revealed that she was born on January 28th. She then celebrated two birthdays, January 27th and January 28th. Did I mention how unique Georgie was?

A week before the planned birthday party, my sons revealed they had set up a fund for their mother. "The Doreen 'Georgie' Mitchell Memorial Fund" was created and would be announced at Georgie's birthday party. The party occurred at J-Roo's restaurant in North Haven, Connecticut, and boy, I was excited! I couldn't wait to celebrate and honor my wife. It was to be a true celebration. We hired D.J. Herman Hamm and had a trivia game created by Greg Bernard, which focused on my wife's life. My sons and I could not play. It would have been embarrassing if I had played and lost. (Just kidding, that wouldn't have happened.) We invited about sixty people. People wanted to come to show their love for Georgie. We wanted people to share their experiences with my wife. My wife kept it real. If she liked you, she loved you. If she didn't like you, she would let you know. My wife was authentic and spoke her mind. I loved her for that. We planned a nice meal, a video slideshow honoring Georgie, and music and dancing after the trivia game and dinner.

The day of the party came, and it was such a lovely day, almost as lovely as Georgie. My heart was overflowing with love and joy. I arrived at J-Roo's restaurant about an hour before the party was scheduled to start to set up the private room where the party was being held. When I arrived, my surrogate daughter, Angela, and her crew (her mom and Shanita) were already setting up. Angela is such a fantastic person. She helped me plan the event and decorated the room to make it special and very personal in honor of my wife. Angela and my wife had a special connection as Angela referred to Georgie as "Mama Mitchell."

The party kicked off, and it was a blast. People couldn't wait to share their stories. Once some guests got their hands on the microphone, they didn't want to give it up. Everyone wanted to tell their story, and then some. Everyone showed love, and it was a special night and celebration in honor of Georgie. Just before the music and dancing, my sons announced the formation of "The Doreen "Georgie" Mitchell Memorial Fund." Everyone wanted to donate to the cause. The money was to be given to a battered women's shelter. Not only did we meet our target goal, which was set a little low at $2000.00, we exceeded it. We presented a check to the shelter for $3000.00 in Georgie's honor. We began planning a cookout at the shelter on Memorial Day, the week of the first anniversary of Georgie's passing. We are doing everything that we can to keep Georgie's memory alive. Did I mention how amazing my sons are?

Chapter Thirteen

# In Loving Memory

Georgie was an extraordinary person. I always knew that she was special, but her passing exemplified this. I always took Georgie's morals, ethics, and values for granted. Since Georgie's passing, I realize that many people do not embody Georgie's values and traits and just how special she really was.

I want my lovely wife to be remembered as a loving soul with a bleeding heart who would stop at nothing to help others. Georgie was a phenomenal mother. She raised and nurtured our three sons, her nieces, nephews, and a host of their friends. Georgie was an incredible wife. Her loyalty, conviction, and "no bull-sh*t" attitude helped to form me as a father, a husband, and a better man. Georgie was loyal as a friend as she was a wife. She was wise beyond her years and as feisty as a bull. Georgie was the person that people turned to when they needed help or wanted a different perspective because she kept it real. She didn't hold back, bite her tongue, or mix words. She told you exactly how she felt.

Georgie was a phenomenal grandmother. The grandkids loved her dearly and could not get enough of coming to "grandma's house." Georgie enjoyed them tremendously during this stage of her life. She lived for the grandkids. Georgie was a very supportive sister. Even though she was the middle child, all her siblings turned to her in their time of need, as if she were the oldest. Georgie was a voice for the voiceless, a defender for the weak, and provided a warm, loving home to all who entered. Georgie was one of a kind. There will never be another like her. I was truly blessed and had the honor of calling Georgie my wife.

Today, I celebrate my wife. I don't mourn her death. Instead, I celebrate the life that she lived. I live for the two of us to tell her story. I will do everything within my power to keep her memory alive. I will always love "My Georgie."

# I Miss You

You were the love of my life, my friend, and my rock.
I MISS YOU.
You are the reason that I get up each day
and go out with a smile.
I CHERISH YOU.
I light up when I meet acquaintances
who acknowledge how special you were.
I LONG FOR YOU.
I hear music that reminds me of you
and the tears start to flow.
I GRIEVE FOR YOU.
You were a very special person,
made just for me.
MY LOVE GROWS FOR YOU.
Today, I live for the both of us, to keep your legacy alive.
I HONOR YOU.
Everyday I look at your pictures all around the house,
and they remind me of how much
I TRULY MISS YOU.
Until we are reunited in eternal love,
I WILL CONTINUE TO MISS YOU.

With all my LOVE,

-Jimmy

## Dedication

This book is written in memory of my darling wife, Georgie—the love of my life. She was the glue that held our family together and made my three sons and me the men that we are today.

Forever in our hearts.

You can help us honor Georgie's memory by donating to ***The Doreen Mitchell Memorial Fund*** at **www.georgieslegacy.com.**

Made in the USA
Monee, IL
30 January 2025

10189695R10035